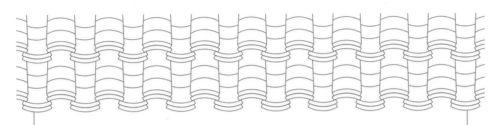

HISTORIC
HOUSES
IN FUJIAN

/////////////////////

• ANCIENT VILLAGES

QU LIMING / CHEN WENBO

福建经典古民居

古村

下

摄影＼曲利明

撰文＼陈文波

海峡出版发行集团
海峡书局

历史的痕迹 / the marks of the history

长洋村全景 / Changyang Village

古田县吉巷乡长洋村

　　长洋村位于宁德市古田县吉巷乡，为中国传统村落。

　　长洋村处于青山环抱之中，一条小溪穿村而过。长洋村历史悠久，村中保存着众多形态各异的古民居，有较高的文化价值。其中以3栋大型古民居最为突出，每栋占地面积600平方米，均为土木结构，房屋门窗、壁板刻有清中期木雕，花鸟和人物栩栩如生，建筑风格古朴典雅。

Changyang Village, Jixiang Country, Gutian County

　　Changyang Village, located in Jixiang Country, Gutian Country, Ningde City, is a Chinese Traditional Village. Being surrounded by the mountains, the village boasts a profound history with a stream tinkling down. Inside the village are a number of different ancient houses with high cultural value. Among these houses, three big mansions are so eye-catching because each of them takes an area of more than 600 square meters. These three mansions are constructed with clay and wood and delicated wood carvings made in the midth of the Qing Dynasty have been well-preserved.

长洋村古民居高大的封火墙，气势壮观 / the high fire wall of the anceint houses

村里至今保持良好的生态，溪水清澈见底 / the clear stream in the village

墙上的捷报和精美木雕 / the reports of vitory and delicate wood carvings on the wall

长洋村大宅 / the mansion in Changyang Village

窗棂风景 / the view at the adjacent of the window

屋脊灰塑 / the grey sculptures at the ridge of the house

垂花柱 / the pillar with swags

精美木雕／the delicate wood carvings

柱础上的风景 / the beautiful stone bases

节孝牌坊 / the memorial arch

凤凰古街 / Fenghuang Ancient Street

古巷深深 / the deep valley

古田县平湖镇富达村

　　富达村位于宁德市古田县平湖镇，为中国传统村落。

　　富达村是闽东历史最悠久、人口最多的畲族村，已有1130多年历史，它是畲族进入闽东最早的迁徙地之一。南宋庆元年间，理学家朱熹曾游览富达村，写下著名的《蓝洞下记》。当年的蓝洞，就是今天的富达村，朱子对富达村喜爱不已，对祠、牛丘、民居等均有细致描述。富达村中，石径相连，房子多为土夯式建筑，古宅之内，雕梁画栋，屋檐之上，精致的浮雕让人眼前一亮。村中还有古井、清代贞节牌坊等古建筑。

Fuda Village, Pinghu Town, Gutian County

　　Fuda Village, located in Pinghu Town, Gutian County, is a Chinese Traditional Village. Fuda Village is a settlement of She's Nationality which has the longest history and largest population in eatern Fujian. It has a history of more than 1130 years and it is the earliest migration spot of She' Nationality in eatern Fujian. In the south Song Dynasty, Zhu Xi who was the famous scholar once visited Fuda Village and wrote an article to describe the beauty of this village. In the article, Zhu Xi made a careful description of the ancestral temple, the mountains and residences in te village. In the village, there is a stone path wandering through and most of the houses were cobs. Within the old residences, one could enjoy the delicate decorations on walls, eaves and beams. Besides these, there are other historic sites such as the old well and the chestity torii in the Qing Dynasty.

时光浸润在石板上 / the stone path taking records of the time

富达村的古民居 / the ancient houses in Fuda Village

石旗杆遗址和别具特色的门楼 / the stone poles and the gateway with local characteristics

蓝公府，供奉富达村先祖蓝文卿夫妇 / Langongfu offering sacrifices to the ancesters of Fuda Village

蓝公府为宋代建筑风格，府内保存有重要牌匾 / Langgongfu being of the construction style in the Song Dynasty

春到小院 / the yard in the spring

精美的垂花柱 / the deilcate pillar with swags

防溅墙上的彩塑 / the colorful sculptures on the wall

屋脊风景 / the view of the ridge of the house

窗棂风景 / the view of the adjacent of the windows

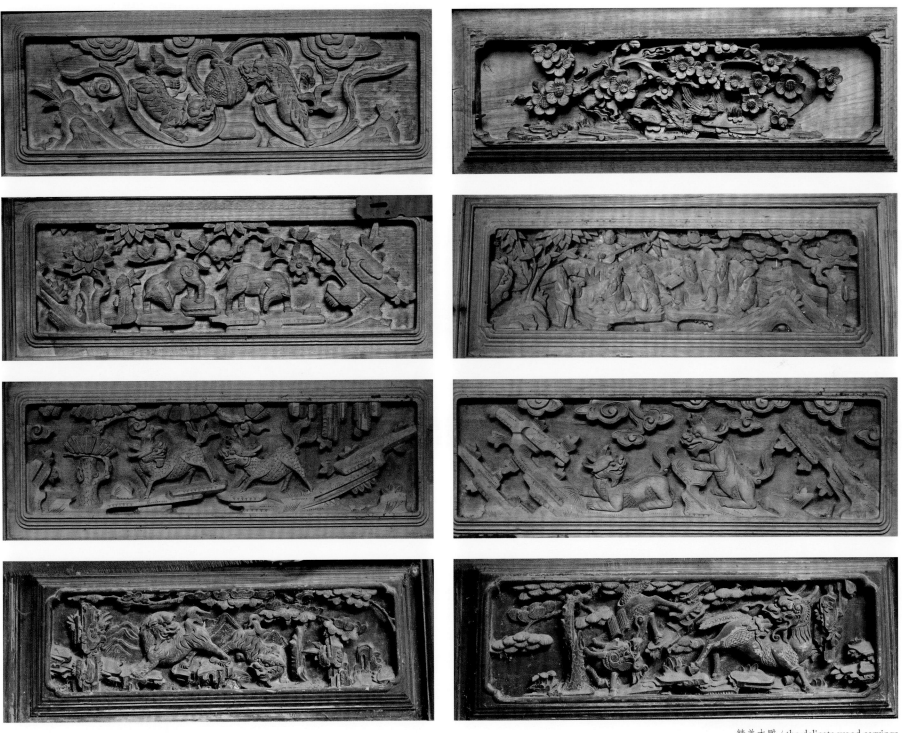

精美木雕 / the delicate wood carvings

竹溪贯穿漈头村，从村头流到村尾 / Zhuxi Stream wandering through the village

深宅 / ancient houses hidden in the alley

屏南县棠口乡漈头村

漈头村位于屏南县棠口乡，为中国历史文化名村。

漈头村历史悠久，始建于唐代，是屏南历史上"四大书乡"的领衔者，曾有"屏南好漈头"之美誉。一条竹溪从山而下，贯穿漈头村，从村头一直流淌到村尾，清澈见底，溪里的鲤鱼，与村人和谐相处。漈头村也是屏南县的大村，人口众多，文风相当兴盛。根据县志记载，漈头村的文风推动了整个屏南县的文化繁荣，在清代中期，也是屏南县科举文化最为发达的时期，行走在漈头村里，一抬头，就能看到"文魁"二字的牌匾悬于门梁或者厅堂之上，翰墨之香满溢全村。

Jitou Village, Tangkou Country, Pingnan County

Jitou Village, located in Tangkou Country, is a Chinese Historic Village. Being established in the Tang Dynasty, Jintou once is the leading goat of Four Book Towns in Pingnan. A stream from the mountain passes through the village. In the clear water, numerous carps are thriving, which makes the village quite well-known. Jitou Village has a large population and a fine tradition of the advocation of education. According to the records, the prosperity of education promoted the overall development of Pingnan County at that time. In the midth of Qing Dynasty, the number of the people who had passed the imperial examinations reached the highest. Walking in Jitou Village, you could spot tablets of Wenkui on the halls even everywhere, which produces an antomsphere of culture.

潦头村的古民居伴水而建 / the residences built along the stream

溪水清澈，溪中鲤鱼与人和谐相处 / the fish and people living in harmony

留守老人 / the empty nesters

潋头村的古民居门楼 / the gateway of the residence

潦头村的古民居门楼 / the gateway of the residence

潔头村的古民居 / the ancient residence of Jitou Village

古民居厅堂 / the hall of the ancient residence

一座廊桥就是一个休闲空间，也是一处神仙府邸，人神同乐 / the gallery bridge being a lounge as well as a temple

精美木雕 / the delicate wood carvings

彩绘木雕 / the colorful wood carvings

民居小品 / the fine work of the residence

祭祀 / the sacrifice

屏南县棠口乡漈下村

漈下村位于宁德市屏南县棠口乡，为中国历史文化名村。

漈下村开基于明代正统年间，至今已有近600年历史。村庄坐东朝西，庐舍依山沿溪构筑，整个村庄周围建起城墙、城门楼、村庄古民居建筑布局成"臼"字形，即活的意思，土匪来时，可四通八达，便于避难和防御。溪水穿村而过，水中鲤鱼成群畅游，人鱼和谐相处。村中现存三座古廊桥，建于清康熙年间的"花桥"最具特色，是全村群众的活动中心。漈下村古建筑颇具特色，名胜古迹甚多，历史文化气息浓厚。这里也是清代名将甘国宝祖居地。

Jixia Village, Tangkou Country, Pingnan County

Jixia Village, located in Tangkou Country, is a Chinese Historic Village. Being established in the Ming Dynasy, it has a history of nearly 600 years. The village is costructed along the mountain. Walls, the arch over the gateway and the old residences were bulit to form a shape that looks like a Chinese character with the meanthing of live. If the village is attacked, people could escape easily with the convenient exits in the village. A stream wander through the village, with various carps swimming happily. There are three old gallery bridges in the village. The one built during the reign of Emperor Kangxi in the Qing Dynasty should be the most outstanding and now it has become the activity center of villagers. Jixia Village boasts a number of historic sites and it is also the original family home of Gan Guobao.

漈下村全景 / Jixia Village

古城、溪水、古民居 / the ancient city, the stream and the ancient residences

溪边四角亭，供奉着关公 / the square pavillion by the stream offering sacrifices to Guangong

还留有时代标语的漈下村老房子 / the old house with slogans on the wall

漈下村古建筑保存较为完整 / the well-preserved ancient architectural complex

漈下村是清代名将甘国宝的故乡，这是甘氏宗祠 / Gan's Ancestral Temple

潴下村的飞来庙 / Feilai Temple in Jixia Village

溪水穿村而过，漈下村的廊桥也有历史 / the gallery bridge with a profound history

这座廊桥叫花桥，是漈下村的活动中心 / Huaqiao having being the lounge of the village

花桥和明代古城门 / Huaqiao and the ancient city gate in the Ming Dynasty

跨过这座廊桥，就算进了漈下村 / after the gallery bridge standing Jixia Village

一座廊桥就是一个休闲中心，供奉一个神灵 / the gallery bridge being a lounge as well as a temple

门 / the wood gate

屏南县双溪镇

双溪镇位于宁德市屏南县，为中国历史文化名镇。

双溪古镇，亦名紫城镇，因南、北双溪交汇本村而得名。发祥于五代后梁，兴建于北宋，鼎盛于清朝道光年间。双溪古镇历史悠久，古代，这里是闽东通往闽北的交通重镇。屏南自设县以来，直到1950年，双溪镇一直是屏南的县治所在，使得双溪镇积累了深厚的历史和文化色彩。现在双溪保存得最完整的老街只有一百多米长，处在镇中心，当年，这是一条商业古街，临街都是店面，黄褐色的木板，透出一丝岁月沧桑，更显几分寂寥。此外，双溪镇还保留有一大批精美的古民居，有陆宅、张宅、周宅、盖屏厝、宋宅等等，尽管风华不再，但从古宅的木雕、砖雕等细节上依然可以管窥当年的风采。

Shuangxi Town, Pingnan County

Shuangxi Town, located in Pingnan County, is a Chinese Historic Town.Shuangxi Town was first established at the begning of the 8th century. It was developed in the Northern Song Dynasty and acheived its prime in the Qing Dynasty. Shuangxi Town is famous for its long history as well as its convenient transportation. Shuangxi Town has been the administrative center of Pingnan county since 1950. Now, there is a 100-meter long old street in the center of the town. In the past, it was a commercial street where shops lined up in the both sides. Besides it, there are also a number of ancient residences such as Lu's House, Zhang's House, Zhou's House, Gaipingcuo House and Song's House. Though the time has gone, people could imagine the glory of those ancient houses from those delicate decorations.

双溪镇老街，曾经是一条繁华的商业街 / Shuangxi Ancient Street being a prosperous business street

双溪镇古民居 / the residence in Shuangxi Village

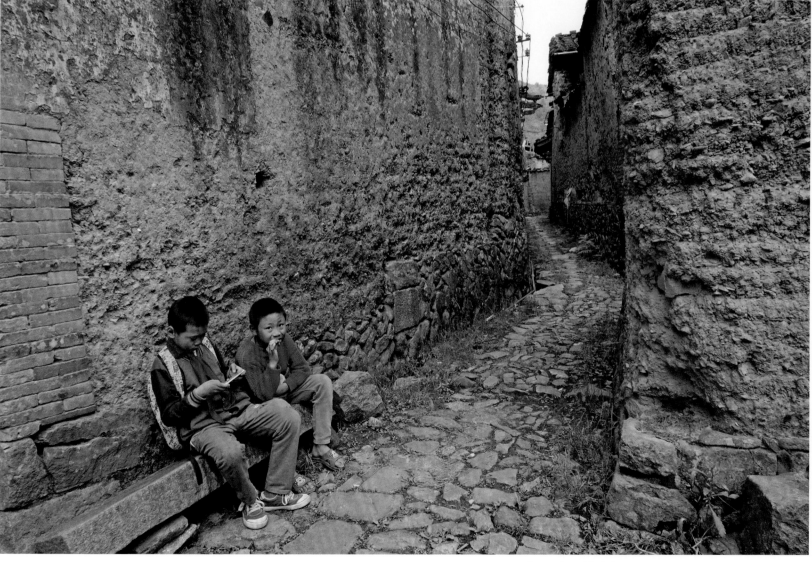

风华不再的双溪镇老宅 / the decayed residences in Shuangxi Village

周氏老宅，双溪镇精美古民居 / Zhou's Ancient house

精美垂花柱 / the delicate pillar with swags

精美木雕和柱础 / the delicate wood carvings and the beautiful stone base

双溪镇的古宗祠 / the ancient ancestral hall of Shuangxi Village

走进时间深处的小巷 / the valley hidden in the depth

屏南县棠口乡棠口村

棠口村位于宁德市屏南县棠口乡，为中国传统村落，福建省历史文化名村。

棠口村，自古以来就是屏南县主要的文化、商业、手工业中心之一。村子始建于宋庆元初年(1195)，迄今已有810多年的历史，悠久的历史，深厚的人文底蕴，让棠口村的名胜古迹众多，有国家级文物保护单位"千乘桥"，县级文物保护单位有"八角亭""祥峰寺""新四军第三支队第六团北上抗日纪念碑"等。

其中千乘桥始建于南宋理宗年间，清代重建。全长62.7米，一墩二孔，整座桥按公鸡形象设计，把正中石墩砌成三角鸡头形，桥面左右为两翼，象征公鸡振翅，昂首报晓。桥中设神龛，祀五显灵官大帝。

Tangkou Village, Tangkou Country, Pingnan County

Tangkou Village, located in Tangkou Country, is a Chinese Traditional Village as well as Fujian Historic Village. From a long time ago, Tangkou had been the cultural, commercial and handcraft center. The village was established in 1195 and it has a history of more than 810 years. The profound history and cultural deposit leave this village with numerous historic sites such as Qiancheng Bridge, Bajiao Pavillion, Xiangfeng Temple and Anti-Japanese Monument. Amongy these, Qiancheng Bridge is the most eye-catching. It was built in Southern Song Dynasty and rebuilt in the Qing Dynasty. With a lengh of 62.7 meters, this bridge is designed to look like a cock. The pier in the middle looks like the head of the cock while the bridge at both sides look like the wing of the cock. The whole bridge does look like a crowing cock. In the bridge stands a shrine honoring Emperor Wuxianlingguan.

八角亭 / the pavillion

祥峰寺和当地的齐天大圣崇拜 / Xiangfeng Temple and the local Monkey King Belief

千乘桥，始建于宋代，重建于清代 / Qiancheng Bridge built in the Song Dynasty and rebuilt in the Qing Dynasty

黄土黑瓦，幽深小巷 / yellow walls and black tiles within the deep alley

状元及第，保存完好 / the well-preserved ancient residence

西浦村是一个具有江南特色的古村落 / Xipu Village

寿宁县犀溪乡西浦村

西浦村位于宁德市寿宁县犀溪乡，为中国历史文化名村。

西浦村历史悠久，文化积淀深厚，自唐以来，人才辈出，先后孕育出状元缪蟾、武状元缪元威等历史名人。村中历史古迹众多，有造型别致的永安桥、太阴宫、状元坊、缪氏宗祠、石门楼、西庵等，是福建省现存历史文物最丰富的村落。西浦村风光秀丽，当地人家大多沿溪而居，溪边古树婆娑，各式桥梁连接两岸，这些桥形式多样，年代各异。其密度为闽东之冠，在福建省也属罕见。

Xipu Village, Xixi Country, Shouning County

Xipu Village, located in Xixi Country, is a Chinese Historic Village. Boasting a profound history and cultural accumulation, the village is the hometown of several celebrities in the past. Inside the village, you could find a lot of historic sites, to name just a few, Yongan Bridge, Taiyin Palace, Zhuangyuan Lane, Miao's Ancestral Temple, the stone gateway and Xi'an Temple. Villgers build their houses along the stream. With dancing old trees and various beautiful bridges, Xipu Village is a wonderful place to visit. Those bridges scattering in the village are built with fine designs in different times. The amount of the bridges in the village is also quite rare in Fujian Province.

缪氏宗祠，造型华丽，雕梁画栋 / Miao's Ancestral Hall with a magnificent mould and fine decorations

缪姓为西浦村大姓，曾出过南宋状元缪蟾 / most of the people in the village bearing the family name of Miao

缪氏支祠，古香古色 / Miao's Ancestral Hall of a certain branch

西浦村古民居沿河而建，造型典雅大方 / the residences built along the river

状元祠，典型的闽东建筑 / Zhuangyuanci House with a typical Eastern Fujian style

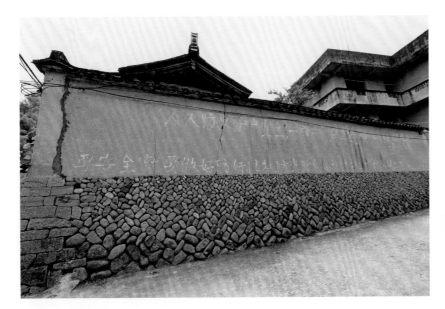

修茸一新的西浦村 / the renovated Xipu Village

太阴宫，始建于元代，供奉三位女性神灵 / Taiyin Palace built in the Yuan Dynasty

精美的藻井和壁画，历经百年风雨 / the delicate sunk panel and the fresco

五显宫供奉五显灵官大帝和土地庙，多神信仰在西浦村很常见 / Wuxian Palace and the sideway shrine

福寿桥，始建于清嘉庆年间 / Fushou Bridge built in the Qing Dynasty

福寿桥内供奉有观音、玄武大帝和临水夫人 / Fushou Bridge offering sacrifices to Kwan-yin, Xuanwu Emperor and Madam Linshui

状元桥，为近年新建 / Zhuangyuan Bridge built in recent years

永安桥，为石板桥，横跨西溪 / Yong'an Bridge over Xixi Stream

上水村全景 / Shangshui Village

上水村土地庙 / the sideway shrine of Shangshui Village

霞浦县崇儒乡上水村

上水村位于宁德市霞浦县崇儒乡，为中国传统村落。

上水村位于霞浦县海拔350多米的山坳中，是较为少见的畲族村寨。村子依山而建，伴溪而生，尤其是，该村传统民居中的石屋寨风格十分独特，是传统畲族村寨石文化的典型代表。今天，上水村还保留有近60座古民居，是目前闽东地区乃至东南地区传统畲族民居保存最完整的村寨之一。漫步在上水村中，石头垒起的几十间村屋，因溪流和地形坡度显得错落有致，古风浓郁。既有南方丘陵地区的山居特点，又有"小桥流水人家"的江南水乡般的灵气。

Shangshui Village, Chongru Country, Xiapu County

Shangshui Village, located in Chongru Country, is a Chinese Traditional Village. Shangshui Village, hidden in the mountains, is a rare village with unique features of She Nationality. The village is unique because of those stone houses which are of typical She Nationality style. There are more than 60 ancneit houses in the village, which makes it the most well-preserved traditional She Nationality village in Eastern Fujian or even the southeast part of China. Strolling in the village, you would find those stone houses scattering in a picturesque disorder along the stream and the slope, which displays features of the mountain occupies as well as the riverside scenery.

上水村是一座建在石头上的村庄，具有典型的闽东畲寨特色 / Shangshui Village being built over stones and of a typical She Nationality style

上水村垒石成村，村中方井，深2米，至今仍在使用 / the square well in the village

厅堂 / the hall of the residence

上水村是石头寨，但古民居建筑核心仍是木材 / most of the residences being constructed with woods

畲族花斗笠以及建筑装饰 / the decorations of She Nationality style on bamboo hats and constructions

山坳里的半月里村 / Banyueli Village in the mountains

霞浦县溪南镇半月里村

半月里村位于宁德市霞浦县溪南镇，为中国传统村落。

半月里村原名"半路里"，是一个纯畲族村落，迄今已有300多年的历史。半月里村山环水绕，村部地形犹如半月，村中环境古朴而静谧。半月里村是闽东地区现存畲族古迹最多的村庄，至今仍保存多座完好的古宅。村中有龙溪宫、雷氏祠堂、举人府等三组清代古建筑和大量畲族文物。

半月里村犹如一座大观园，是福建省畲族绵延发展的缩影。在这里，时光如梦，人人都是文化遗产的"传承人"。

Banyueli Village, Xinan Town, Xiapu County

Banyueli Village, located in Xinan Town, is a Chiense Traditional Village. Banyueli, also called Banluli in the past, is a She Nationality village which has a history of more than 300 years. The village looks like a half-moon. Roaming in the village, you could savor the tranquility and profound history at the same time. Banyueli is a village that boasts the most historic relics of She Nationality in Eastern Fujian. Inside the village, lots of ancient house are preserved in fine conditions. Longxi Palace, Lei's Ancestral Temple and Juren House are three ancient architectural complexes built in the Qing Dynasty. Banyueli Village displays the development of She Nationality in Fujian.

半月里村为典型的闽东畲族村 / the village with typical She Nationality style

半月里村还保存有成片古民居 / the ancient residences

村中也留有大量的夯土建筑 / the cobs in the village

别具特色的半月里村古民居 / the ancient residence

雷氏宗祠，地处半月里村核心位置 / Lei's Ancestral Temple

龙溪宫，供奉畲民信仰的薛元帅等神祇 / Longxi Palace offering sacrifices to the gods of She Nationality

周宁县纯池镇禾溪村

禾溪村位于宁德市周宁县纯池镇，为中国传统村落。

禾溪古称 "湫溪"，以溪为名，解放后 "湫" 字去 "水" "火" 更名为 "禾溪"。该村位于芹山水库之滨，村中一弯清水穿溪而过，村民临水而居，黄墙黑瓦的古屋高低不同，却错落得匠心独具。飞檐翘角，在阳光的照耀下，处处彰显着这个千年古村的凝重与祥和。禾溪村开基于明代，村中历史文化古迹众多，其中木拱廊桥 "三仙桥"，始建于明成化三年(1467)，距今已有500多年历史，为中国已知现存建造时间最古老的木拱廊桥，已被列入《中国世界遗产预备名单》。

Hexi Village, Chunchi Town, Zhouning County

Hexi Village, located in Chunchi Town, is a Chinese Traditional Village. The village, situated at the side of Qinshan Reservoir, has a clear stream wandering through. Villagers build their houses along the stream. The ancient houses with yellow walls and black tiles are arranged in picturesque disorder. The raising eaves under the sunshine display the tranquility of the tiny village. Being established in the Ming Dynasty, the village boasts a great number of historic sites. Among those, Sanxian Bridge, the gallery bridge built in 1467, is the oldest wooden gallery bridge known to the nation. Now the bridge has been listed in the Preparatory Directory for World Cultural Heritages of China.

保生宫 / Baosheng Palace

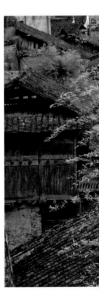

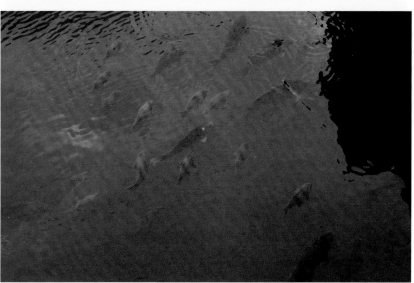

禾溪村生态良好 / the fine ecological environment of Hexi Village

禾溪村沿溪建村，高大的夯土古民居蔚为壮观 / the magnificent cobs along the stream

禾溪村不大，一条小溪就是村子的活动中心 / the stream being the activity center of the village

窗外的禾溪 / Hexi Stream

廊桥、古民居，构成一幅古香古色的画面 / the gallery bridge and the ancient houses composing a picture with antique flavor

三仙桥始建于明代，桥中供奉着三位仙姑 / three goddesses built in the Ming Dynasty being honored in Sanxian Bridge

叩响湖头 / Visiting Hutou Town

安溪县湖头镇

　　湖头镇位于泉州市安溪县，为中国历史文化名镇。

　　湖头镇四面崇山环抱，一水拖蓝中分阆苑，因地形颇似大湖，古称"阆湖"，北宋初称湖山，南宋年间朱熹路经此地雅称"湖头"至今。湖头镇历史悠久，文物古迹众多，有国家重点文物保护单位李光地的宅与祠，此外，镇上还有保存较为完好的明清古民居建筑群60多座。湖头镇历来是安溪县的交通枢纽和商贸重地，素有"小泉州"之称。

Hutou Town, Anxi County

　　Hutou Town, located in Anxi County, is a Chinese Historic Town. Being surrounded by mountains, the landform looks like a big lake. In the Northern Song Dynasty, it was called Hushan. The famous scholar Zhu Xi of the Southern Song Dynasty passed here and addressed it with a more elegant name, that is, Hutou. Therefore, the name passes down from that time. The town has a pround history, a bunch of cultural relics and historic sites including Li Guangdi's House and Ancestral Temple. Besides these, there are more than 60 ancient houses in the town. Hutou, being called as Small Quanzhou, is a commercial town and a transport hub in Anxi County.

湖头镇全景 / Hutou Town

湖头镇古民居 / the ancient houses in Hutou Town

湖头镇的古民居多为闽南红砖厝 / the red-brick houses of Southern Fujian style

红砖厝上的装饰色彩艳丽 / the colorful decorations

清代名臣李光地府邸新衙，又称昌佑堂 / Changyoutang House

修葺一新的昌佑堂，为五进院落，门庭广阔。堂内悬挂的牌匾均为御赐 / the renovated Changyoutang boasting large space

湖头镇李氏家庙，又称李氏大宗祠，为四进院落 / Li's Family Temple with four yards

湖头镇三平观 / Sanpingguan in Hutou Town

湖头镇有多个李光地故居 / various former residences of Li Guangdi

李光地祠中的石碑亭，立有御碑 / the pavillion in Li Guangdi's Temple

泰山岩，是安溪镇三大历史名岩之一 / Taishan Rock

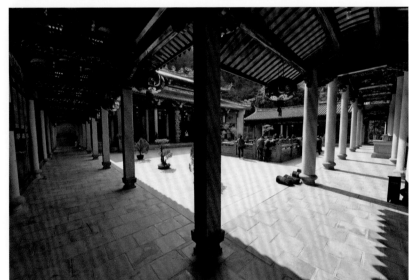

泰山岩香火旺盛 / Taishan Rock being a popular honoring place

雕梁画栋的泰山岩寺庙群 / the temples at Taishan Rock

问房大厝，湖头镇的明清古建筑 / Wenfang House

高大的宅院，失去了往日的喧嚣 / the huge house now being empty and quiet

精美柱础 / the delicate stone bases

永春县岵山镇

岵山镇位于泉州市永春县，镇上共有茂霞村、塘溪村、铺上村、铺下村等4个村子入选中国传统村落。

岵山镇是闽南地区遗存保留较为完整的千年古镇，这里传统民居保存完好，生态良好，镇子还被列入闽南文化生态保护区规划中的历史文化村镇保护区域。岵山镇有着从明代留存至今的闽南传统民居350多座，其中保存完好的有80多座；有迄今400多年历史的石砌古寨福茂寨，还有石城寨、草铺城、水瓢寨等古寨；有百年荔枝树1800多株，更有一对树龄500年的夫妻树……古街、古厝、古镇、古树与田野相互交错，山水相依，是都市人释放压力、寻找"乡愁"的好去处。

Gushan Town, Yongchun County

Gushan Town, located in Yongchun County, is a well-preserved ancient town in Southern Fujian. Maoxia Village, Tangxi Village, Pushang Village and Puxia Village are on the list of Chinese Traditional Village. Inside the town, one could easily spot those fine traditional residences. Because of its excellent natural environment, this town is also listed as a conservation area. There are more than 350 traditional residences of Minnan Style, among which 80 houses are in fine conditions. Old villages such as Fumaozhai Village, Shichengzhai Village, Caopucheng Village and Shuipiaozhai Village are worth of a visit. Besides those villages, there are some old trees in the town. More than 1800 lychees are over 100 years old. A couple tree of 500 years is hidden somewhere. The old street, old houses, old towns, old trees and the farmland are arranged in a picturesque order. It is a wonderland for citizens to take a break and savor the happy moment in the wild.

岵山镇全景 / Gushan Town

闽南气息浓郁的岵山镇 / Gushan Town of Southern Fujian style

和塘老街，一条以骑楼为主的商业街 / Hetang Ancient Street

岵山镇古民居，为典型的出砖入石的闽南红砖厝 / Gushan residences

在岵山镇，随处可见闽南红砖古厝 / the red-brick houses in Gushan Town

峣山镇南山陈氏宗祠 / Chen's Ancestral Temple

燕尾脊、红砖厝，闽南味十足的古村 / the swallow-tail spinals and the red-brick houses

古厝精美垂花柱 / the delicate pillar with swags in the ancient house

福兴堂，闽南传统建筑中的奇葩 / Fuxing Hall

福兴堂又称李家大院，建于民国时期，至今已有70多年历史 / Fuxing Hall, also called Li's Hall, being built at the time of the Republic of China

福兴堂至今仍有4户李姓后人居住 / Li's offsprings still living in Fuxing Hall

精美木雕 / the delicate wood carvings

精美垂花柱／the delicate pillar with swags

福兴堂中木构件全为手工打造，相当精美 / Fuxing Hall being made with human work

做工精细的木构件，为闽南罕见 / the delicate wood structure

精美木构件 / the delicate wood structure

精美石雕 / the delicate stone carvings

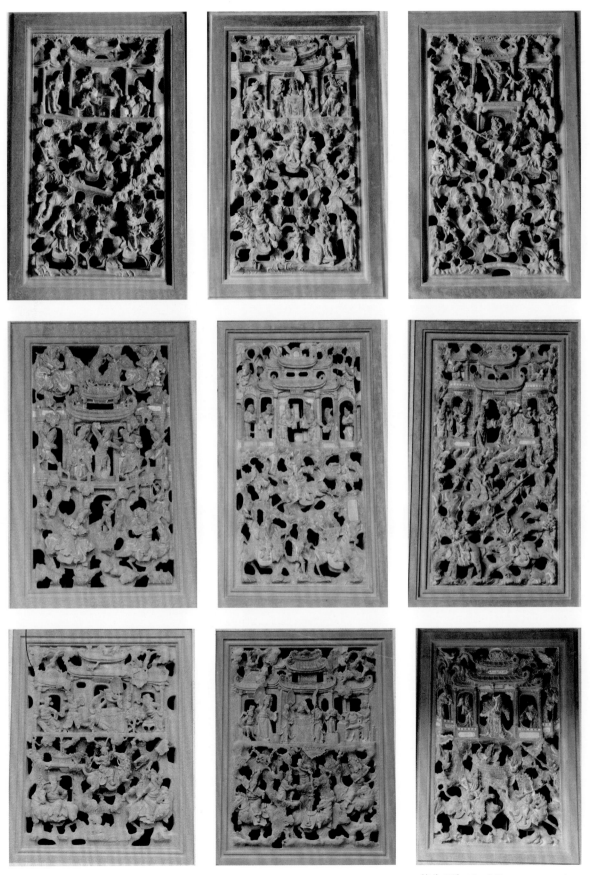

精美石雕 / the delicate stone carvings

柱础 / the stone base

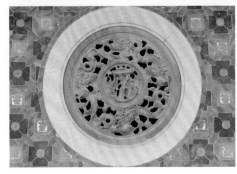

墙上风景 / the view on the wall

屋脊风景，精美彩塑 / the delicate colorful sculptures at the ridge of the house

屋脊风景，精美彩塑 / the delicate colorful sculptures at the ridge of the house

精美彩塑 / the delicate colorful sculpture

古寨也是峇山镇的时代印记 / the ancient stockaded village being the mark of the times

荔枝是岵山镇特产，在古镇随处可见荔枝树 / Lychees being the specialty of Gushan Town

典型的岵山镇古民居 / the typical Gushan residence

城镇化建设中的古宅 / the ancient house in the urbanization

岵山人家，处在核心位置的神龛 / the shrine in the core of the house

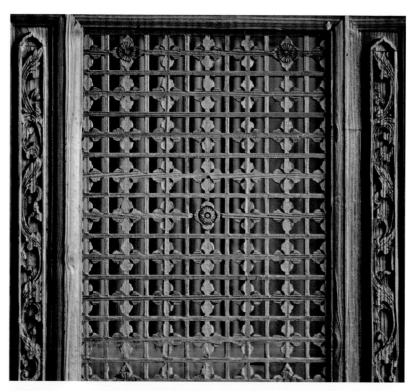

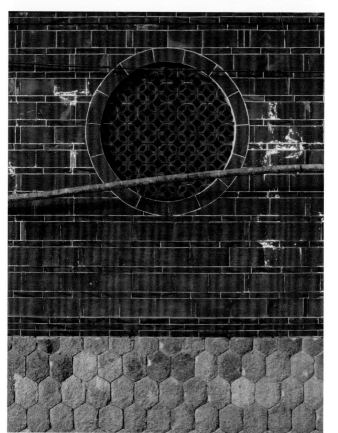

精美雕刻 / the delicate carvings

闽南人家，烟火气息 / the family in Southern Fujian district

坚守在老宅中的老人 / the old man living in the old house

神龛 / the shrine

厅堂里的神龛 / the shrine and the hall

闽南人家门额上往往标有堂号 / the name of the house being carved at the door

精美木雕 / the delicate wood carvings

精美木雕 / the delicate wood carvings

墙上风景 / the view on the wall

防溅墙上的彩绘 / the colorful painting on the wall

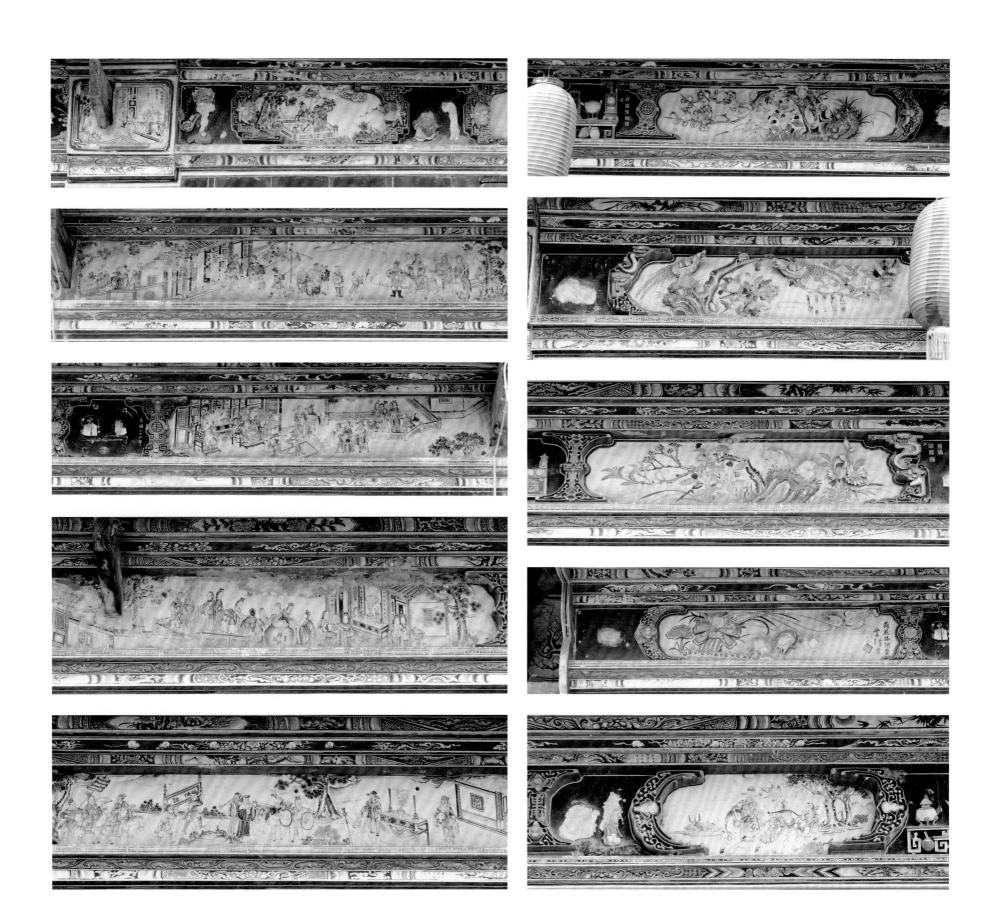

有故事的壁画 / the fresco telling a story

壁画 / the fresco

融合了南洋风格的岵山镇古民居 / Gushan residence with the cosntructing style of Southeast Asia

骑楼下的工夫茶，闽南人家的日常生活 / drinking tea under the sotto portico

用石柱代替木材，实用的建筑理念 / replacing the wood with stone pillars being very practical

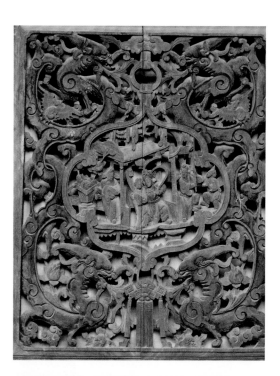

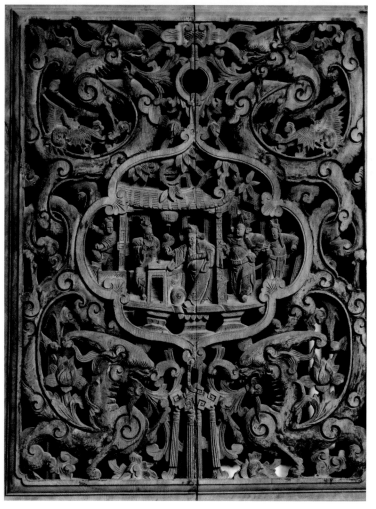

工艺繁复的精美木雕 / the delicate wood carvings

防溅墙上的彩塑 / the colorful sculptures on the wall

西陵宫，供奉武安尊王 / Xiling Palace offering sacrifices to Wu'anzunwang

南音演奏，岵山镇保留着丰富的非物质文化遗存 / Nanyin – the intangible cultural heritage in Gushan Town

天堂宫妈祖庙 / Heavenly Goddess Temple

土地庙 / the sideway shrine

仙游县石苍镇济川村

济川村位于莆田市仙游县石苍镇，为中国历史文化名村。

济川古名"漈坑"，又名济水，是一个有着两千多年历史的古村落。济川村地处仙游县、永泰县交界，古时仙游入永泰，就经过济川村，迄今还留有一条千年古道。村内风光秀美，历史古迹众多，在济川村，有三古宫、三古亭、三古桥、三古树、三秀山、三古寨、三古井等，而且村里还保存着"为有楚歌杂吴谣"的十音乐队和木偶戏班子。此外，村中还有明清壁画、寨保山门、古行驿道、旗杆夹石、爱云石碑、古代瓦窑等古迹，村里的历史文化景点竟超过百处。

Jichuan Village, Shicang Town, Xianyou County

Jichuan Village, located in Shicang Town, is a Chinese Historic Village. Jichuan Village, also called Jikeng and Jishui, has a history of more than 2000 years. Since it is located at the juncture of Xianyou County and Yongtai County, there is an ancient path in the village. The pictureque village boasts numerous historic sites including Sangu Palace, Sangu Bridge, Sangu Tree, Sanxiu Mountain, Sangu Village and Sangu Well. In the village there is a local band and a puppet troupe. Frescos, the old gateway, the ancient path, the stele and the old tilery are traces of the times. More than 100 historic sites could be found in this tiny place.

天堂宫妈祖庙是济川村的重心 / Heavenly Goddess Temple being the center of Jichuan Village

上坪村人的日常生活 / the daily life of the family

上坪村全景 / Shangping Village

建宁县溪源乡上坪村

上坪村位于三明市建宁县溪源乡，为中国传统村落、福建省历史文化名村。

上坪村，处在山间盆地中，历史上曾名六龙井、楚下堡。走进上坪村，如同走进历史画卷，前年古驿道从村中穿过，遥想当年，这里是明清时期闽赣省界驿站，商贾云集，繁盛一时。今天，村子至今完好地保留有杨氏家庙、杨氏社主庙、杨家学堂等古建筑26幢，最早建于宋代后期，大多为清代建筑。上坪村大部分姓杨，相传为杨家将后人，家族崇文尚学，历代儒风不衰。

Shangping Village, Xiyuan Country, Jianning County

Shangping Village, located in Xiyuan Country, is a Chinese Traditional Village and Fujian Historic Village. This villge, also called Liulongjing and Chuxiabao, is right in the basin of the mountains. Strolling in Shangping Village is like walking in a historic picture. The ancient path wanders through the village. In the past, it is the posthouse at the border of Fujian and Jiangxi in the 17th century where lots of merchants would gather to trade their goods. Until now, those ancient buildings inculding Yang's Family Temple, Yang's Study are preserved very well. The earliest buildling could date back to the end of the Song Dynasty. Most of those old buildings are built in the Qing Dynasty. Most of the villagers in Shangping Village bear the family name of Yang and are said to be the offsprings of generals of Yang's Family in the Song Dynasty. Villagers advocate education and study throughout the time.

上坪村曾繁盛一时，如今只剩古建筑的门楼依然伫立 / the gateway of the ancient house revealing the glory in the past

门楼依然伫立 / the standing gateway pasting throuth the times

"空心化"侵蚀村落，村中只剩留守的老人和小孩 / the empty nesters and the left-behind children

古桥，走过商贾，走过士子，也走过岁月 / the ancient bridge witnessing the times

传统的大灶，和岁月一起老去 / the traditional oven being aging with the time

厅堂和悬挂起来的历史 / the hall and the hanging history

杨氏家庙，建于清乾隆年间 / Yang's Family Temple

五谷殿，上坪村的民间信仰 / Wugu Palace—a local folk belief in Shangping Village

木板房是肖家山村的主流建筑 / wooden house being the major architectural building in the village

肖家山村全景 / *Xiaojiacun Village*

明溪县胡坊镇肖家山村

　　肖家山村位于三明市明溪县胡坊镇，为中国传统村落。

　　肖家山村历史上是明溪通往永安的必经之地，历史悠久，文化底蕴深厚，人文景点众多，至今仍保存明清及民国时期的古驿道、古廊桥、古门楼、古碉堡、古民居等古建筑。肖家山村生态优越，是闽江支流鱼塘溪、胡贡溪、九龙溪的"三溪源头"，村子有众多的峡谷、急流、瀑布，境内动物、植物资源十分丰富，是天然的"森林氧吧"。

Xiaojiashan Village, Hufang Town, Mingxi County

　　Xiaojiashan Village, located in Hufang Town, is a Chinese Traditional Village. In the past, it is the only way connecting Mingxi County and Yong'an County. Since it has a profound history, there are lots of historic sites in the village including the ancient post road, the old gallery bridge, the old gateway and the old residences. Xiaojiashan Village also has a fine natural environment since it is located at the headstream of Yutangxi Stream, Hugongxi Stream and Jiulongxi Stream. There are valleys, rushing streams and waterfalls around the village. Various plants and animals could be found around it and it is a natural oxygen bar.

肖家山村古民居、古井 / the residence and the old well

留守老人 / the empty nesters

在山村，祠堂永远是最气派的建筑 / the ancestral temple always being the most magnificent buidling in the village

天井、厅堂，空无一人 / the lonely yard and hall

始建于宋代的月峰寺，历经多年重修，香火旺盛 / Yuefeng Temple built in the Song Dynasty

月峰寺供奉有定光佛、观音等神灵，为客家地区的重要信仰 / Yuefeng Temple being the place for some important gods of Hakka people

肖家山村的水尾廊桥 / Shuiwei Gallery Bridge

水尾廊桥内有周武公镇妖神像，有乡规民约的石碑 / the statue of Zhouwugong and the stele with folk regulations

岩前村全景 / Yanqian Village

宅院门楼 / the gateway of the residence

宁化县安远镇岩前村

岩前村位于三明市宁化县安远镇。

岩前村地处安远南部，这里是闽江源头村之一，村子在武夷山脉最南麓，紧挨福建省省级自然保护区牙梳山森林公园，风景秀丽，具有独特的地文景观和丰富的生态资源。

Yanqian Village, Anyuan Town, Ninghua County

Yanqian Village, located in the south of Anyuan Town, is the village of the headwater region of Minjiang River. The village, at the southern foot of Mount. Wuyi, is near Yashushan Forest Park which is a provincial natural reserve. The village boasts a beautiful landscape, unique scenes and abundant biological resources.

木板房是岩前村常见的古民居 / wooden houses being common residences in the village

谷仓 / the barn

岩前村依山而建，木材是当地最主要的建材 / wood being the major building material

岩前人家 / the family in Yanqian Village

厅堂 / the hall

阳光照进天井，午后的岩前宁静安详 / the yard under the warm sun

传统农具，一代又一代使用至今 / the traditional farm tools

赵家源全景 / Zhaojiayuan Village

独轮车 / the wheelbarrow

宁化县安远镇赵家源

　　赵家源是个自然村，位于三明市宁化县安远镇东桥村。

　　安远镇是个历史悠久的文明古镇，宋称"黄土岗"，并建"下土寨"，设监巡官。到了明代，废寨改置为"安远司"，之后几度兴废，直延至清，民国时期改为安远镇。赵家源就在安远镇的东桥村，村中至今保留着古老的生活方式，鲜见现代建筑，李氏家庙，为清代建筑，造型奇特，有较高的价值。

Zhaojiayuan Village, Anyuan Town, Ninghua County

　　Zhaojiayuan Village, located in Dongqiao Administrative Village, is a place with profound history. In the Song Dynasty, the village, also called Huangtugang, built a stockaded village. In the Ming Dynasty, the stockaded village was changed to Anyuansi. During the reign of the Republic of China, it was changed to Anyuan Town. Zhaojiayuan Village is within the area of Dongqiao Administrative Village. In the village, people still carry on their traditional life style and few modern building could be found. Li's Family Temple, which is built in the Qing Dynasy, is of great historic value.

乡村生活气息浓郁的古村落 / the ancient village with a strong smack of everyday life

赵家源普通民居 / the common residence in the village

厅堂 / the hall

用报纸贴墙，曾是乡村时尚的做法 / the wall pasting with newspaper

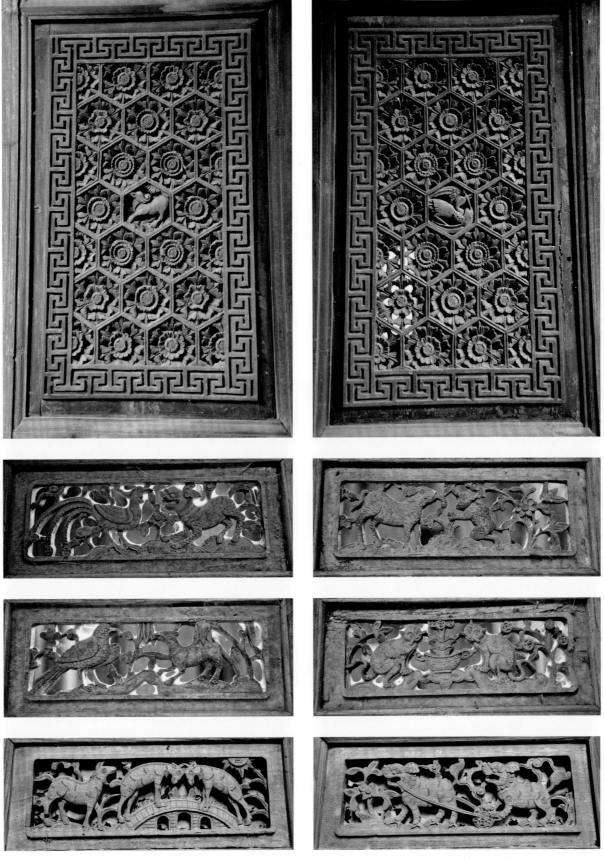

窗棂风景 / the view at the window

只剩下老人的村庄 / the village with empty nesters

建于清代的李氏家庙 / Li's Ancestral Temple builted in the Qing Dynasty

神龛 / the shrine

宁化县曹坊镇下曹村

　　下曹村位于三明市宁化县曹坊镇，为省级历史文化名村。

　　下曹村始建于南宋德祐元年（1275），距今已700多年的历史。村中共有古民居45座，大多建于明末清初，建筑时间长的约有四五百年，最短的也有二百多年。走进下曹村，仿佛让人误入时光隧道，回到百余年前的古村落。下曹的古民居是典型的客家建筑，为"九厅十八井"构造，特别是"杨岗公祠"和"敬湖公祠"至今还完好保存着罕见的清代室内古戏台。

Xiacao Village, Caofang Town, Ninghua County

　　Xiacao Village, located in Caofang Town, is a Fujian Provincial Historic Village. Being establised in the Southern Song Dynasy, the village boasts a history of more than 700 years. There are 45 ancient residences in the village and most of them are built at the end of the Ming Dynasty or the beginning of the Qing Dynasty. The oldest house is built at 400-500 years ago, even the newest one is built at 200 years ago. Walking in Xiacao Village, you would feel like taking a walk in the past. Those residences are typical Hakka buildings which are composed of nine halls and eighteen yards, especillay the well-preserved Yangganggongci and Jinghugongci.

下曹村全景 / Xiacao Village

下曹村老人 / the old men in Xiacao Village

古民居东山拱秀 / the ancient house—Dongshangongxiu

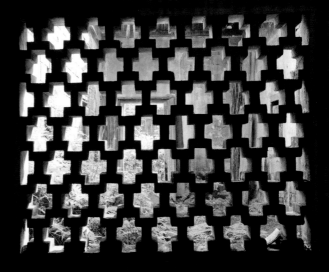

雕花窗棂，岁月留痕 / the delicate adjacent of window

保存完好的古建筑敬湖公祠 / Jinghugongci—the well-preserved ancient ancestral hall

古戏台，每年庙会，这里都会请戏，酬神敬祖 / the old stage

曹氏宗祠，雕梁画栋，富丽堂皇／ the grand and delicate Cao's Ancestral Hall

曹氏宗祠，近年来重新整修 / Cao's Ancestral Temple being renovated in recent years

赖坊镇风水树 / the geomantic tree of Laifang Town

赖坊镇全景 / Laifang Town

清流县赖坊镇

赖坊镇位于三明市清流县，为中国历史文化名镇。

赖坊镇以古建筑群规模大、保存完好著称，古建筑群主要集中在镇政府所在的赖安、赖武和南山三个古村落，古村主要以明清时期客家村落骨架的街巷、完整的水网系统布局、交通、商贸、学校、城门等社会性基础设施和宫庙祠堂、祖屋、古民居等保存完整、有序分布，堪称古代闽西客家建筑的"活化石"。赖坊镇古民居中，木雕、砖雕、石雕等为主的"三雕"艺术也相当出彩，图案设计精到，技法娴熟，基本还保持着当时的风貌。

Laifang Town, Qingliu County

Laifang, located in Qingliu County, is a Chinese Historic Town. It is famous for the large-scale ancient architectural complexes which are protected quite well. The ancient architectural complexes are in Lai'an Village, Laiwu Village and Nanshan Village. Those architectural complexes are comprised of Hakka style streets, alleys, rivers, social infrustructures, temples, ancestral houses and residences. All these buildings are well arranged in different part of the villages and preserved the original look of Hakka architectural complexes in Western Fujian. The wood carvings, brick carvings and stone carvings of Laifang's ancient residences are eyecatching beacuse of their delicate design and marvellous craftmanship.

古民居彩映庚 / Caiyinggeng House

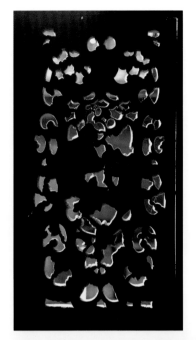

精美窗棂、垂花柱 / the delicate adjacents of windows and pillars

古民居来青，取青气东来之意 / Laiqing House

招贴画，时代的印记 / the poster with the memory of the past

窗棂风景 / the view at the window

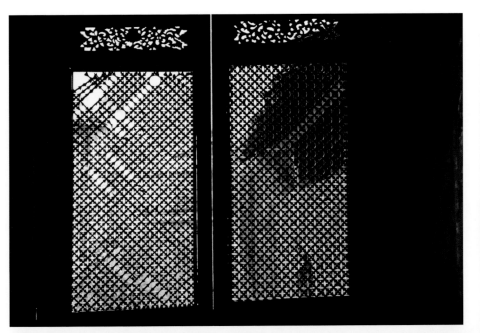

窗棂风景 / the view at the window

宗祠门楼上的雕花风景 / the view on the gateway

赖坊镇的马氏宗祠 / Ma's Ancestral Hall

赖坊镇本土神庙 / the local temple offering sacrifices to the folk belifs in Laifang

文昌溪上文昌桥 / Wenchang Bridge over Wenchang Stream

忠山村又名十八寨 / Zhongshan Village (Shibazhai Village)

三元区岩前镇忠山村

忠山村位于三明市三元区岩前镇，为中国历史文化名村。

忠山村的核心在十八寨，相传是由大大小小的18个寨子组成的，因此而得名。

现有保存完好的唐、宋、元、明、清古建筑二十余座，民间还流传着许多具有丰富文化内涵的传统民俗。今天，走进村子的深处，会发现一条用光洁的青灰条石铺就的古街，这就是"蜈蚣街"，始建于元代，总长470多米，贯穿全村。街两旁多是明清时期的民居，走在古香古色的街巷中，不由激发怀古之幽思。村落中古老的建筑群掩映于群山绿树的疏影中，各式各样的老房子，保存良好的多是元、明、清时建造的：四贤祠、庄氏宗祠、楚三公祠、杨氏三公祠、陈家祖屋、万安桥、文昌阁、蒙古墓……

Zhongshan Village, Yanqian Town, Sanyuan District

Zhongshan Village, located in Yanqian Town, is a Chinese Historic Village. The core area of Zhongshan Village is at Shibazhai which is comprised by 18 stockaded villages. Within the village, you could spot ancient residences built in the past and the traditional folk customs with rich cultural connotations. An old street named Wugong Street is paved with boulder strips, which was first built in the Yuan Dynasyt. On both sides of this 470 meter long street are a number of old residences built in the Ming Dnasty or the Qing Dynasty. It certainly would triger your memory when roaming in the street. Those old houses hide in the forest and mountains, creating a visual feast for people. Sixianci House, Zhuang's Ancestral Temple, Chusangongci House, Yangshisangongci House, Chen's Family House, Wan'an Bridge, Wenchang Pavilion and Menggumu are all in fine condition waiting for your visit.

忠山村保留有大量的明清古建筑 / the ancient buildings in Zhongshan Village

长达一里的蜈蚣街，国内罕见 / the 500 meter-long Wugong Street

明代古桥万安桥 / Wan'an Bridge built in the Ming Dynasty

清同治年间的古建筑楚三公祠 / Sangongci built in the Qing Dynasty

耕读传家是忠山村的传统 / education and farming being the tradition of the village

精美木雕 / the delicate wood carvings

窗棂风景 / the view at the window

窗棂风景 / the view at the window

宗祠门前石旗杆，科举时代的象征 / the stone pole before the ancestral Hall—a signal in the age of imperial examinations

无碍斋，当地神明急脚尊王的办公地 / Wu'aizhai—the temple of a local god

永兴庵，供奉急脚尊王的地方 / Yongxing'an Temple

先贤祠，又名四贤祠，供奉杨时、罗从彦、李侗和朱熹 / Xianxianci Temple (Sixianci Temple)

吉山村 / Jishan Village

永安市燕西街道吉山村

吉山村位于三明市永安市燕西街道，为中国历史文化名村。

抗日战争期间，福建省省会内迁永安达七年半之久，而吉山村作为省政府主要机关及大专院校的驻地，至今仍保留着多处抗战文化旧址。永安抗战旧址群被列为第七批全国重点文物保护单位，大部分抗战旧址均在吉山村。吉山村村子坐落在文川溪下游，一条大河绕村而过，养育了这一方水土，也让这里的风光、生态都保持得很好。吉山村不显山露水，却历来崇文尚武。明末以来经济发展，文化繁荣。清朝康乾时期更是盛极一时，当时书斋林立，文人辈出，至今已有300年历史，萃园书院就是吉山村书院的代表。

Jishan Village, Yanxi Street, Yong'an City

Jishan Village, located in Yanxi Street of Yong'an, is a Chinese Historic Village. During the Anti-Janpanese War (1937-1945), Yong'an was the provincial city then and Jishan Village was the site of some key departments and colleges. Therefore, inside the village, you could find a lot of historic sites. These historic sites are listed as the 7th Key National Protection Units. The village is embraced by Wenchuan Stream which nurishes the villagers and the beautiful landscape. Though the village is hidden in the corner, villagers here are advocaters of both literature and martial arts. In the Ming Dynasty, with the development of economy, the culture also developed quite rapidly. Till the Qing Dynasty, studies and bookmen were common scene in the village. Cuiyuan Study with 300 years old is the typical representative in Jishan Village.

历史上吉山村曾盛极一时，古建筑鳞次栉比 / the ancient architectural complexes

吉山村保留大量的清代古建筑，抗战时期，这些建筑都曾作为福建省政府各部门驻地 / the ancient houses being used as offices of the government during the Anti-Japanese War

吉山村古建筑 / the ancient houses in Jishan Village

萃园书院，清代建筑，为吉山村保存最为完好的古建筑 / Cuiyuan Study built in the Qing Dynasty being the most well-preserved ancient building in the village

书院曾培养出100多位进士、举人和秀才 / the study being the birthplace of scholars and celebrities

修葺一新的萃园书院 / the renovated Cuiyuan Study

吉山村的抗战标语，提醒人们这里曾有过的硝烟 / the Anti-Japanese Slogan

吉山村刘氏宗祠 / Liu's Ancestral Hall

宗祠门前的石旗杆 / the stone pole before the ancestral hall

宁静安详的古村落 / the village in tranquility

残破的窗棂，岁月无情 / the wrecked adjacent of window being the mark of the times

吉山村宝应寺 / Baoying Temple

溪水环绕吉山村，溪边的民主公王庙和浮桥 / the temple and bridge at the bank of the stream

尤溪县洋中镇桂峰村

　　桂峰村位于三明市尤溪县洋中镇，为中国历史文化名村。

　　桂峰村已有700多年的历史，开基始祖为北宋名臣蔡襄之后，其第九世孙蔡长。桂峰整个村庄均依山就势而建，分布于村中的三面山坡上，层层叠叠，错落有致。据考证，现存39幢古建筑群中，最早的建于明代后期，数量最多的则是清初建筑。村里有数百株四季桂花，常年芳香四溢，漫步其中，宛如穿越时空。当年，这里是闽西北通往福州的必经之地，在最繁华的时代，这里酒肆、客栈林立，有"小福州"之美誉。

Guifeng Village, Yangzhong Town, Youxi County

　　Guifeng Village, located in Yangzhong Town, is a Chinese Historic Village. Being established by Cai Chang who is the 9th generation of Caixiang—the famous chancellor in the Northern Song Dynasty. The village is built along the mountains, scattering on the slopes. These houses are arranged in picturesque disorder. According to certain research, the earliest building among the 39 ancinet architectural complexes is built in the 1640s. Most of those ancient houses are built in the early Qing Dynasty. Inside the village are a number of osmanthuses which give out elegant fragrance all year round. Once upon a time, Guifeng Village, used to be the route connecting Fuzhou and Western Fujian, was called little Fuzhou because it was as prosperous as the real one.

桂峰后门山大厝 / Houmenshan Big House in Guifeng Village

桂峰村曾经繁华一时 / the prosperous Guifeng Village

印桥皓月，桂峰八景之一 / the moon over Yinqiao Bridge—one of the eight scenes in Guifeng

蔡氏宗祠，桂峰村蔡氏为宋名臣蔡襄后人 / Cai's Ancestral Hall

蔡氏宗祠 / Cai's Ancestral Temple

宗祠门前的石旗杆，诉说当年繁华 / the stone pole in front of the ancestral hall telling a story of the prosperity

宗祠内的牌匾，彰显蔡氏在科举时代的辉煌 / the tablets inside the ancestral hall showing the glory of the Cai's offsprings

信步走来，就是一栋大厝 / the ancient house

精美石雕、柱础 / the delicate stone carvings and stone base of the column

墙上风景 / the view on the wall

精美灰塑 / the delicate clay sculpture

大山深处的村庄 / the village in the depth of the mountain

吊脚楼、木板房，彩洋村的建筑全部取材于大山 / the building material being obtained from the mountain

尤溪县西滨镇彩洋村

彩洋村位于三明市尤溪县西滨镇。

彩洋村地处尤溪县最高峰莲花山下，交通不便。近年来，随着村民渐渐搬出大山，彩洋村人口越来越少，所以全村几乎看不到新建的房屋，反而保存了古村落的原始和宁静。彩洋村里留存的房屋，建筑年代都不长，多是砖木结构。彩洋村每年最热闹的就属三月三了，在外的游子基本都会回归到这个小村庄，庆祝节日，祈祷来年。

Caiyang Village, Xibin Town, Youxi County

Caiyang Village, located in Xibin Town, is under Lianhua Mountain which is the highest mountain in Youxi County. Since it is located in the depth of mountain, the transportation is not so convenient. In recent years, villagers leave the place to earn their livings in cities, leaving only few people. Because of the increasing job-hunting people, few new house are built. Luckily, it leave the village in tranquility and its original look. Most of the houses in the village are made of bricks and wood. The most busy day in the village should be the 3rd day in Lunar March when youngsters return to celebrate the local festival.

彩洋人家 / the family in Caiying Village

每年三月三，彩洋村都会举行盛大的游神活动 / the god parading festival held on 3rd Lunar March

人们祭祀神树，欢聚一堂 / people worshiping the sacred tree

将乐县万全乡良地村

　　良地村位于三明市将乐县万全乡，被列入首批中国传统村落和第六批中国历史文化名村名录。村子虽然偏远且小，但是一个具有千年历史的传统村落，小小的村子中，有文武庙、梁氏宗祠、绪蜒厝、月山公屋、后恢谷仓和水尾木廊桥等省级文物保护单位。良地村虽然历经上百年的风雨，但至今完整地保留着由庙、祠、宅、仓、桥等各类建筑组成的良地村古建筑群。其中，该村粮仓遗址大小共12处，这种大面积集中兴建一处的社仓群属我国少见。

Liangdi Village, Wanquan Country, Jiangle County

　　Liangdi Village, listed as the First Chinese Traditional Village and the Sixth Chinese Historic Village, is a traditional village with a history of more than thousands of years. Even it is hidden in the depth of the mountain, there are various provincial historic sites such as Wenwu Temple, Liang's Ancestral Temple, Xuyancuo House, Yueshangong House, Houhui Barn and Shuiwei Gallery Bridge. Even it has gone through such a long time, the village still preserved a serious of architectural complexes. Among all these buildings, the 12 barns in the village are the most outstanding sicne it is very rare to build this big group of barns in such concentrated area.

文武庙 / Wenwu Temple in the village

良地村全景 / the overall view of Liangdi Village

良地村的古建筑古朴典雅，保存完好 / the well-preserved ancient residences in Liangdi Village

良地村依山而建，展示了山地古村落独有的原生态景观 / Liangdi Village builted along the mountain

良地村古民居多为土墙、青砖造就，村子内巷弄相连，都是石铺小径，别具美感 / the beautiful ancient houses made of cobs and bricks

静静的良地村 / the tranquil village

城市化的进程中，良地村人大多外出，只剩下安静的古厝 / the ancient houses in quietness

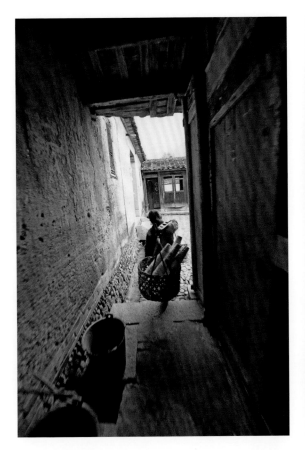

月山公屋 / Yueshangong House

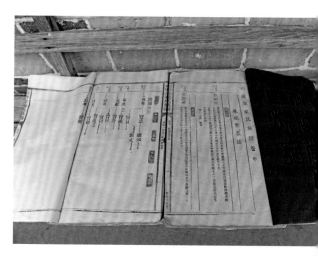

保存完好的宗祠和族谱显示，良地村有近千年的历史 / the well-preserved ancestral temple and the family tree

文武庙始建于明末，乾隆二十六年(1761)重建。分上下两层楼，上祀孔子，额题"文教昌明"，下祀关公，额题"圣之义者" / Wenwu Temple built in the Ming Dynasty honoring Confucius and Guangong

水尾廊桥，横跨良地溪，始建于清初，清咸丰七年(1857)重修 / Shuiwei Gallery Bridge over Liangdi Stream

桥廊里建有六个神龛，分别供奉如来、真武帝、妈祖、许真人、萧公尊王、本坊土地福德神 / Shuiwei Gallery Bridge over Liangdi Stream

大源村福塘 / Futang Pond in Dayuan Village

泰宁县新桥乡大源村

　　大源村位于三明市泰宁县新桥乡，为中国历史文化名村。

　　大源村历史悠久，这里位于闽赣接壤之地，自古就是交通要道，特别是在清朝时，这里成为闽赣之间重要的贸易通道，村子因此鼎盛一时。村里的古民居大多依山而建，层层递高，青砖黑瓦与山林之景相互映衬，透露着山地民居的朴素与典雅。大源村分上大源、下大源两个自然村，逐渐形成了两个古建筑组群，即上大源村的南溪庙、文昌阁、三圣庙组群，以及下大源村的隆兴庙、永安殿、奎星阁组群等，至今保存完好。

Dayuan Village, Xinqiao Country, Taining County

　　Dayuan Village, located in Xinqiao Country, is a Chinese Historic and Cultural Village. Once upon a time, it was an important route since the village was at the juncture of Fujian and Jiangxi. It was an key trade route connecting Fujian and Jiangxi, therefore it was quite prosperous in the Qing Dynasty. Most of the ancient residences are built along the mountains. The colorful bricks and tiles brighten the view in the depth of the mountains, revealing the elegance of the ancient houses. Been divided into two natural village—Shangdayuan Village and Xiadayuan Village, it boasts two groups of ancient architectural complexes. There are two different architectural groups in the village. All those buildings are in fine conditions under careful protections.

大源村地处青山绿水的环抱中 / Dayuan Village surrounded by green hills and clear water

靠山吃山，木材是大源村最重要的资源 / wood being the major resource of Dayuan Village

厅堂，神龛摆放在古民居最重要的位置 / the shrine being placed at the most important place of the residence

寂寥的古村落 / the lonely village

青砖黛瓦，古老和现实 / the grey bricks and black tiles

雀替和柱础，可以管窥当年大源村的繁华 / the decorated brackets and the base of column

建于清雍正年间的文昌阁 / Wenchang Pavillion built in the Qing Dynasty

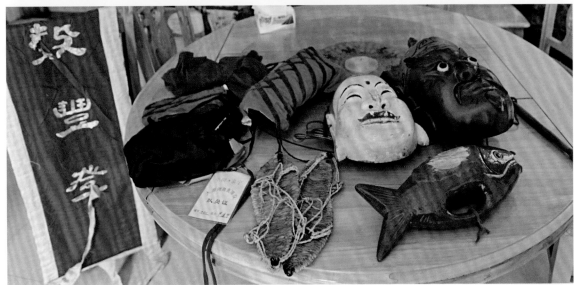

大源村傩舞是省级非物质文化遗产 / Luowu Dance of Dayuan—the intangible cultural heritage of Fujian Province

建于清康熙年间的戴氏宗祠，是大源村古民居的代表 / Dai's Ancestral Temple built in the Qing Dynasty

镇安桥，当年行旅人必经之路 / Zhen'an Bridge – the only way of travellers in the past

魁星楼、古桥、古庙 / Kuixing Building, the ancient bridge and the ancient temple

大源村盛产竹笋，当地竹笋加工形成一条龙产业 / the bamboo shoot processing industry being prosperous in Dayuan Village

长泰县马洋溪生态旅游区山重村

　　山重村位于漳州市长泰县马洋溪生态旅游区内，为中国传统村落，也是著名的旅游村落。山重村原名三重，因为村子地处偏僻，面对三重山、三重水而得名。古时，山重村交通不便，如今，随着旅游的开发和与厦门一山之隔的地理优势，山重村已经成为闽南著名的旅游村落。

　　今天的山重村有上万亩的果园，是漳州市面积最大的梅、桃、李种植地区。每年春节前后，万亩梅花、桃花、李花盛开，繁花似锦，美不胜收。此外，村中还保存着大量的闽南古厝，走进古村，鹅卵石铺路，巷道相交，仿佛穿越时空。山重村春节期间，还有著名的赛大猪民俗活动，成为当地的一大看点。

Shanchong Village, Mayangxi Stream Tourist Zone, Changtai County

　　Shanchong Village, located at the tourist zone of Mayangxi Stream of Changtai County in Zhangzhou, is a Chinese Historic Village and a famous tourist attraction. Since it is located in a remote place which faces the mountains and rivers, it was named after Sanchong which meas a remote place in Chinese. In the past, it is inconvenient to go outside. Nowadays, with the development of tourism industry, the village has now been famous.

　　In Shanchong Village is a large area of fruit plantation where a great many of plums and peaches are growing. During the Spring Festival, Shanchong is the most beautiful village because of the prosperous blossoms. Meanwhile, there is one more thing to attract the attentions of tourists, that is , the ancient houses. Walking in the village on the pebble roads, one might feel travel back in times. What's more, a great event of the pig competition would be held during the Spring Festival. It is also a great view that one would not want to miss.

老宅大多空巢，现代建筑从四周拔地而起，留存的老屋成了文物，给当地的经济带来收益 / most of the empty ancient residences being listed as cultural relics by the local government, bringing certain profits for the place

较早的老宅，除白灰部分脱落，依然保存完好 / the well-preserved ancient residence with peeling limes

石板水池，延续了利用石材的传统方式 / the stone water basin being a new way to use stones

555

闽南沿海的老屋，瓦片比常见房屋密度要大，石材料坚实如新，木质基本破损 / larger tiles, strong stones and broken wooden structure being frequent views of the ancient residences by the coastal region at Southern Fujian

鹅卵石与麻石搭建的老宅，冬暖夏凉，天然淳朴 / the ancient house built with pebble stones and granites offering comfortable living environment for residents

飞檐翘角的屋檐装饰 / the decorations of the eaves

"文化大革命"时期的建筑标志 / the symbol of "Cultural Revolution"

昭灵宫，建于明嘉靖年间，宫内浮雕、彩绘、透雕，形式多样，内容丰富 （郑友亨摄）/ Zhaoling Palace, built at the Jiajing Period of the Ming Dynasty, boasting a variety of fine arts such as relief carvings, colorful paintings and openwork carvings (Photoed by Zheng Youheng)

屋旧人离去，老藤依故里 / the empty old house decorated by old vines

千年古樟，历经沧桑，依然生长旺盛 / the old camphor tree being full of vigor

卧樟，被一次台风刮倒，依旧生机盎然 / the falling camphor being vigorously alive

水尾塔，始建于宋末整个塔为鹅卵石砌成圆锥形七层台阶式的实心塔，占地面积155平方米，高8.45米，塔刹造型独特，与佛教有关（那兴海摄） /
Shuiwei Tower, built at the end of the Song Dynasty, being a seven-floor solid coniform tower with an area of 155 square meters and a height of 8.45 meters
(Photoed by Na Xinghai)

百余幢红瓦老宅，排列整齐，保存完好 / the well-preserved ancient residences with red tiles lining up in the village

龙海市东园镇埭美村

　　埭美村位于漳州龙海市东园镇，为国家级历史文化名村，也是中国传统村落。村子始建于明朝景泰年间，至今已有560余年的历史。由于村子四面环水，埭美村又被称为水上古民居，是目前漳州市规模最大，保存最为完整的古民居建筑群，被誉为"闽南第一村"。

　　埭美村尽管是古民居建筑群，但村子布局合理，井然有序，村落为埭美先人统一规划，统一建筑，全村共有276座古厝，均为传统的闽南硬山式燕尾脊红砖厝。漫步村中，随处可见的古民居坐向，形态、大小近乎一致，若无引导，很难分清方向。古民居为典型的闽南红砖建筑，屋顶以曲线燕尾式为脊，室内木雕精细，梁上漆画清晰可辨，虽经风雨侵蚀，仍保存完整。

Daimei Village, Dongyuan Town, Longhai City

Daimei Village, situated at Dongyuan Town of Longhai in Zhangzhou, is a state-level historic and cultural village. The vilage, established in Jingtai Era of the Ming Dynasty, boasts a history of more than 560 years. Since the village is surrounded by water, it has obtained a name as the ancient residences by the water. It is the largest and most well-preserved ancient architectural complex in Zhangzhou and cowned as the No.1 village in Southern Fujian District.

Though this village was built a long time ago, it is well-arranged and delicately designed by the ancestors of Daimei villagers. There are 276 ancient residences which are all built in the same style using red bricks with swallow-tail spinal. Wondering in the village, you might easily get lost since the residences all look the same in size, direction and design. These old residences are carefully decorated with wood sculptures and lacquer paintings which have gone through times.

门前风光无限 / the marvellous landscape in front of the house

古宅与新厝，干净整洁，排列有序，厝与厝相互间距1.5米左右 / the old residences and new houses being allocated in harmony, the residences being built with a clearance distance of 1.5 meters

蓝天碧水，鸟语花香，一幅"水上古民居"画卷 / a fine scroll of ancient resideces by the water

千年"三角梅"古树，难得一见 / the rare Bougainvillea spectabilis with a history of 1000 years

古榕树下的妈祖庙，多了不少的灵气 / the Mazsu Temple under the old banyan tree

三十米宽的水道绕村而过 / a river with about the width of 30 meters wandering along the village

树倒不死，绿叶终年不衰 / the falling tree still bearing green leaves all year round

腌制咸菜的生活场景 / making pickles being a daily life of the villagers

闽南建筑以暖色基调为主，院内花卉也不例外 / the application of warm tone being the major feature of Southern Fujian Style residences

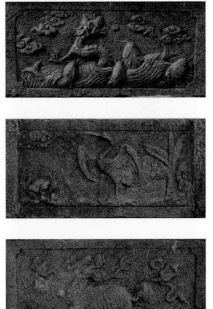

前祠堂，始建于明末清初的官厅 / Qiancitang Hall – a formal hall builted in the midth of the 16th century